Why is it that the best
is always one more

... from what one is being?

Greetings, Mawson. We are Seekers.
We travel far and wide, Seeking.

How exciting. I once set off Seeking too.

What did you go seeking for?

Umm ... what was it for now?
Oh yes, for Me!

Did you find you,
Mawson?

Oh my
goodness, yes.

But I don't
remember now
where I was.

Hello, Mawson.
Did you hear that
dreamy music?

Hello, Samantha.
Umm, what music?

I was sure I
nearly heard it
before it slipped
away.

It was like the colours of the wind singing sadly.

Or like the sighing of forgotten names still longing to be heard.

It was too soft for me, Sam.

My Ponders
Attempt only One Nap at a time.
Don't Skip those In-Between Naps.
Too many Naps ? How ??
Nap and grow Plump.
The Best Time to Nap is after the One Before.

I dream of being a **king**, Mawson.

I'd do mighty deeds.
And everyone would say ...

'There goes King Scotland The Brave.'

Or, you could be our very own Scottie
just the way we love you.

I suppose so.
But it's not the same.

Pile up Your
Cushions
and
the **Naps**
Will Take Care
of Themselves.

Professors Caddy and Bree, hello.
Is this your latest creation?

Quite so, Mawson. We have changed this
wishing lamp. Now it is for Wish-Backs.

Many of our wistful friends wish
for what they want.

But when some rue their whimsy they
can't wait to wish their wish <u>back</u>.
Our Lamp is for them.

A Wish-Back-Lamp, Professors?

We've high hopes for it, Mawson, high hopes.

Maybe today ...
I'll see the moon
fall through the
window like a lost
orange.

And maybe today
I'll make a new
friend, like a tiny
dragon. I'll call him
Drago.

Mmmm. Oooof.

And my dragon will kindly
fly the moon back to the sky.

Oooomp. Errrgh.

So many wonders could happen today.

That's why every day is grand, Sam.

A Nap
is a
Holiday
from
Bothers.

What's Prof Bree making now, Caddy?

It's our Fault-Finder, Mawson.
Let's test it on you.

We start the Broinger, thusly. Then blip the Gizfong. Next, we whirly the Glooper. The Da-Plonker will go "plunk".

Then we can read out all your faults. Strange! What! Bother!

Is it broken, Professor?

It's saying you have no faults!

How disappointing. And it looked like a splendid Fault-Finder.

We had high hopes for it, Mawson, high hopes.

Mawson, you know that moment just before you dance?

I'm not sure I ever danced, Samantha.

There you are, ready to dance.
And out there, just beyond your paws ...

... wait all the dances of the world ...

... calling you to step out
into them.

Wouldn't it be wonderful to always
be there, in that very moment,

just before you dance.

I dream of being a great guitarist, Mawson.

But Scottie, you don't
know how to play.

No, but I will bravely improvise.

Eeeeeeeeaaaaiiiiiiiiii

It's a long waaaaaayyyy

Brrrrrooaaaggkkkeiieeeee to the bed

If you wanna fall asleep!

It's our Hope-Maker, Mawson.

Hidden in each Hope is a Happening,
you see, that wants to hop out.

But when a hoper stops hoping,

the Happening can't happen - it's held in.

Our Hope-Maker here makes simple little hopes to help hopeless hopers practice their hoping.

It sounds grand, Professors.

We have the highest hopes for it, Mawson.

I'm on my way to bed, Mawson.
Beautiful dreams are waiting for me.

I'll put them in my treasure box.

Are the dreams happy to
join your treasures, Sam?

Oh yes. Dreams like their dreamers to keep them safe and hold them tight.

We have returned, Mawson,
from Seeking far and wide.

We found a place between myths
and memories ...

... Where shadow-poems flutter,
waiting to be written,

And stories wonder who will make them true.

Now the kindly paths least travelled are
turning us for home.

Oh My
Goodness!

Samantha,
what is it?

Oh, Mawson, I had a
sudden feeling that ...

... Everything ...

... is ... All Right.

Lightning Source UK Ltd.
Milton Keynes UK
UKHW020707290121
377891UK00003B/18

9 781922 311139